High Tide, Full Moon and Fading Memories

High Tide, Full Moon and Fading Memories

● ● ●

Julie Ann Rumbold

ISBN-13: 9781539012917
ISBN-10: 1539012913

This book is dedicated to my grandparents, Lilian and Wade Rumbold, and to my parents, Ronald and Maura Rumbold, and to all the previous residents of Thompson's Beach and East Point.

Contents

Acknowledgments

● ● ●

I AM GRATEFUL TO NUMEROUS people who helped in the development of this book by sharing their time, stories, memories, and pictures with me over the last couple of years. Their fondness for Maurice River Township, and particularly Thompson's Beach and East Point, quickly became clear to me. What we all had in common was a shared love story. None of us wanted the memories to be lost in time. There are many people to thank, and they include Bettie Archie, John Barone, Kim and Kristen Barone, Vic Ballato, Skip DeGlavina, Ronald Flynn, Chick Foster, Bob Frantz, Dakota Hafer, Bill Hawn, Sharon Johnson, Nelson Klein, Ed Krupa, Karen Lee, Christina Longley, Ryan McClellan, Louis and Kit Peterson, Amy Smith, Richard and Rick St. Aubyn, Drew Tomlin, Tom and Lyn Wiechnik, and Adam and Megan Valenzano. The Grace of God and support of friends of Bill W. paved the way. I am also most grateful to the Maurice River Township Heritage Society and Friends of East Point Lighthouse for their tireless efforts to preserve the area and its history.

Introduction

• • •

As my husband sometimes says, fairy tales start with "once upon a time," while hero stories begin with "no shit—there we were…" I can tell you there were many instances of hero stories at Thompson's Beach and East Point over the last several decades. In the following pages, you will read accounts of several such events. So grab a cup of coffee and a warm cookie, sit back, and enjoy.

For those readers who are not familiar with this part of New Jersey, Thompson's Beach and East Point are in Maurice River Township in Cumberland County, south of the cities of Vineland and Millville. For shore travelers, these places are off Route 47. In the past, most shore traffic to Wildwood and Cape May utilized Route 47, which is also known as the Delsea Drive.

Back in the 1930s and 1940s, people would travel from the larger cities and come to stay by the bay in the hot summer months. At that time, there were over one hundred homes at Thompson's Beach along with several boat rental places, cottages for rent, and a couple of restaurants. Access to the ocean beaches in this era was more limited. The Bayshore area drew crowds because of thriving shipbuilding, glass manufacturing, and oyster industries in the surrounding villages and towns.

A devastating storm hit in November of 1950. Some insurance companies classified it as a tidal wave. Many area residents refer to it as the Flood. It occurred because of a combination of unfortunate events, including a full moon, relentless winds, and exceptionally high tides. Thirteen people in the vicinity lost their lives. Most of the homes floated from their moorings and into the surrounding salt-hay meadows or out to sea. Most of the residents did not return. A few brave souls risked resettling the beach. My grandparents and great uncle and aunt were among the ones who took a chance.

I spent every summer of my childhood at Thompson's Beach. My parents added a cottage next to my grandparents' place in the early 1960s. My family loved that place. Some of my best memories are from leisurely summer days near the bay.

In the fall of 2013, my husband and I bought a camper-type cottage at the neighboring beach of East Point, where my sister, brother-in-law, and nephew already had vacation places. As we reminisced about the good old days, it occurred to me that not many people even knew about these beach communities and that if the stories were not gathered and written down, they would be lost to time. I decided to start interviewing former residents of Thompson's Beach as well as current residents of East Point and surrounding towns. As I spoke with people and listened to their stories, I realized the loyalty and deep love people have for the region. I hope readers will come to love this area as well.

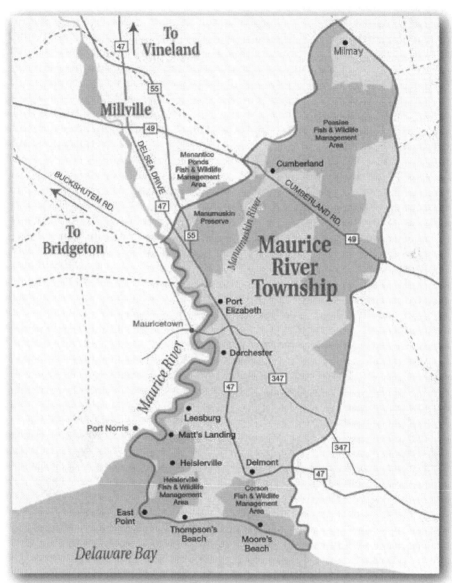

This is a map of Maurice River Township including Thompson's Beach and East Point. (Courtesy of Maurice River Township).

Thompson's Beach Stories

● ● ●

High Tide, Full Moon and No Escape

THERE WE WERE, THE SUMMER residents of Thompson's Beach, at high tide with a full moon and no way out. What used to pass for a crooked, well-worn gravel road seemed to have morphed into a raging river. Unfortunately, as I recall, this was often the case in the mid- to-late 1960s, when sections of road at Thompson's Beach in Heislerville, New Jersey, regularly washed out with the tide. In those days, dump trucks delivered piles of colorful slag glass and concrete to serve as barricades against the water, but the towering buffers could do only so much to hold back the unrelenting forces of nature.

High tides and strong winds often propelled the water, forcing it through crevices and weakened areas in the protective piles of rock. Several times beach residents needed to drive cars through fast-moving, rapid currents of water that raged across the gravel road. I remember being afraid as a teenager of either being stuck or being swept away by the current. With my knuckles turning white, I would tightly grip the steering wheel and lean forward in the front seat, concentrating and praying to make it through to the other side of the raging water. Traveling through the overflow was especially frightening when it was dark, and the wind was driving the water in stormy conditions. When this happened, the headlights were the only illumination, and once the car was in drive, and I was up to the wheel wells in water, there was no turning back. I had to keep forging ahead. Gravel washed away, tires churned slowly through soft sand, and we sometimes wondered if we would get through. Locals knew there was

1

never a guarantee that we would make it safely to or from the beach when conditions were so precarious, and we lived much of our summer lives bayside according to the schedule of the tides, moon, and storms. After all, things could always be worse when the moon was full, and the tide was high. Some of the worst storms occurred in those conditions.

MONSTERS AT THOMPSON'S BEACH

Thompson's Beach residents liked to party. This tradition dated back to the 1930s and continued until the last of the residents were forced to leave when the beach officially closed in the late 1990s. This particular story is one from long ago in the late 1940s. Back then, the residents always had an end-of-season party on the beach in September, and hundreds of people would attend. One year, however, attendees experienced a very unusual, unexpected, and terrifying event.

As night fell, the crickets were chirping while revelers were enjoying their food and drinks and sitting around bonfires scattered along the beach. The adults were roasting their hot dogs and sipping their beers. People were relaxed and enjoying the party atmosphere as they entertained themselves and one another by recalling humorous neighbor stories of summers gone by and stories about who caught the biggest fish and the one that got away. The children were getting tired. Their hands were sticky from roasting marshmallows, and they were starting to whine. Some of the kids were running along the water's edge. Suddenly, three hideous and frightening creatures that looked a lot like Frankenstein and a couple of deformed monsters lurched toward them from the waters of the bay. The children ran screaming to their parents. Stories passed down through the generations recall that people freaked. One man grabbed a burning log from the nearest bonfire and hurled it at the monsters as they approached, burning his hand in the process. Chaos ensued.

After the initial panic, the monsters removed their masks to calm people down. It so happened that the beasts from the bay were actually three residents dressed in scary costumes. According to longtime area resident Nelson Klein, the creatures were actually his grandfather Adolfe Klein; his father, Nelson Klein Sr. (Frankenstein); and a neighbor, Herman Di Polito. It was a beach party people wouldn't soon forget!

The three monsters who lurched from the bay turned out to be from left to right Adolfe Klein, Nelson Klein Sr. and Herman Di Polito. All of them were Thompson's Beach residents. (Courtesy of Nelson Klein).

THE BEACH CURE

Probably my first real sense of the connectedness of God with nature, came to me as I walked along the beach as a child. What a wonderful treat for the senses it was. It seemed that nothing came close to the feeling I got when wiggling my bare toes in the hot sand and feeling the blanket of warmth from the sun wrapping about my young shoulders. If I listened closely, I could hear sounds of the waves lapping on the shore and the squawking of the seagulls above. When I took a deep breath, my lungs would fill with the wonderful smells of the salt air.

I spent countless days, walking the shoreline between Thompson's Beach and East Point. My dog, Whiskers, often accompanied me and seemed to thoroughly enjoy rolling in every dead, stinking creature he could locate and chasing sandpipers and seagulls to his heart's delight. Consequently, there were many dog baths when we returned to the cottage.

I remember times when I would set out on a walk when something was troubling me. It never failed that concerns would fall away as my little feet made ongoing impressions in the sand. Strolling along the beach always brought about stillness, peace, and tranquility in me. Although I didn't understand it at the time, being near the water was good for my soul.

It may sound strange to people who didn't grow up spending summers on the bay, but I also loved to walk through the mud that was ever present near the salt-hay marshes, and feel it squishing between my toes. Sometimes I would sink up to my knees and spend some time trying to pull my legs out of the deep gray mud.

Depending on how early or late it was in the summer, I sometimes encountered thousands of horseshoe crabs or saw tiny turtles hatching from their eggs and making their journey to the sea. I once stepped on a horseshoe crab tail and got quite a foot puncture wound. I ended up having to go the doctor's for antibiotics when a red line started up my leg.

I spent hours searching for and collecting seashells, sea glass, driftwood and colorful stones. I also became an expert at chasing minnows and splashing them up onto the sand from shallow pools of water at low tide just for the sport of it. They would always wiggle their way back into the safety of the bay. I was quite contented on the beach.

I spent June to September mostly barefooted. The skin on my feet would become quite calloused walking on the gravel road in front of the houses and on the sandy beaches. I remember walking on a lit cigarette without dire consequence to show people how tough my feet were.

It seems that those beach-walking summers of my youth rolled by so slowly, as time tends to go when you are young. I wouldn't trade the Thompson's Beach years for anything. They contributed to some of the happiest times and memories of my life.

Louis and Kit Peterson's Recollections

● ● ●

Deep Roots

Louis Peterson was born in Bridgeton Hospital during a snowstorm on Christmas morning 1935. He has been married to Kathryn (Kit) Peterson—the aunt of Russell Sachleben III, a friend of my nephew Ronnie's—for sixty-one years. Russell was kind enough to arrange an interview with his aunt and uncle, who live in Heislerville, New Jersey, and have deep roots in the area. Kit and Louis met on the school bus as teenagers and started dating when Louis was a teenager and working for Kit's father, bringing boats in and preparing them for customers at his boat rental place at Thompson's Beach.

When Kit was about thirteen years old in 1950, her family had a house at Thompson's Beach for a short period. Kit remembers that there were beautiful houses with lovely grass-filled yards and plentiful trees. Her family moved away in October, because Kit's mother was afraid to stay at the beach alone—and a devastating storm struck the town the following month. If they hadn't moved back to Erial, New Jersey, early, they may have been casualties in that fateful storm.

Louis's parents moved to Heislerville from the town of Port Norris, across the Maurice River, with his grandfather who worked in the oyster business, which was thriving at the time. Louis's parents moved into his grandparents' house, known as the Block House, on East Point Road after his grandparents relocated to another home. Locals called the building the Block House, since a family named Block had operated a saloon there prior to selling it. The county was a dry one that did not sell alcohol.

Several speakeasies, or saloons, in the area quietly served alcohol. Louis's grandparents moved from the Block House to the Station House on Matt's Landing Road. The town had built a railroad station there to compete with the railroad on the other side of the river at the town of Bivalve. The town planned to transport oysters out of the area by the carloads to restaurants and wholesalers. At that time, there was a road through the woods that stretched from East Point Road to Matt's Landing Road. Louis would walk with his mother and brother Fred to his grandmother's house via this path. The Block House burned down circa 2011.

Erosion in the area has been happening for many decades. In fact, Louis's grandfather Aaron Peterson told him that during his lifetime, the land by the water at East Point and Thompson's Beach had eroded one thousand yards. That would have been in the early to mid-1900s.

The Stack Yards

Louis recalls that he used to go to Thompson's Beach to Adolfe Klein's store to buy ice-cream cones in the 1940s, and he remembers the "stack yards" on the East Point end of Thompson's Beach. These were huge stacks of salt hay in the meadows behind the beach. The Thompsons, who managed the salt-hay meadows, would store the stacks there once they were harvested. Per Louis, the stacks spanned great distances and had spaces between them. Every Fourth of July, the townspeople of Heislerville would head down to the stack yards. They would cook hot dogs, and the kids would go swimming to cool off in the hot summer. People would change their clothes between the haystacks. Louis joked that these spaces were "spy territory" for some of the young boys and girls, who would watch people change into their swimsuits.

Russ's Rowboats

Kit told my sister, Tina, and me that her dad, Russell, bought land from Roland Butcher that was on the right-hand side of the road as you entered Thompson's Beach. According to Louis, Roland had bought the land from George "Bonesy" Thompson, a descendant of the Thompsons for whom the beach had been named. In the 1930s and 1940s, Mr. Thompson operated an establishment there that was a decent-size inn and a store.

Kit's dad built a store, because nothing remained after the storm in 1950. He called the store, which he owned from about 1953 to approximately 1967, Russ's Rowboats. Kit said Russ's Rowboats had a bait house on the bay side; a long pier; and many boats, which the family rented to the area's numerous fishermen. Louis stated that the bulkhead was at least another fifty feet out toward the water then. On the other side of the street sat a restaurant that served hamburgers and clam chowder for lunch and sold breakfasts to the fishermen.

This is a photograph of Kathryn Sachleben in 1955 posing in her cap and gown for her high school graduation. She is standing on the pier at her father's place of business, Russ' Rentals, at Thompson's Beach. (Courtesy of Kit Peterson).

The *Henry Clay*

When Louis Peterson's grandfather Aaron bought an oyster boat called the *Henry Clay*, it had a cracked shaft. Aaron decided to repair the damage himself and tore out the pilot house—which meant there was no floor. According to Louis, Aaron just put a couple of planks down and worked on the boat from right there.

Louis said his grandfather was a very smart man. When World War II started, Aaron recognized that boats were becoming motorized. He told his sons they should get boats and join the trend, because he recognized that when boats became powered, fishermen would collect oysters more quickly and, at some point, would "kill" the bay by overharvesting. Aaron helped Louis's father, Fred, by buying the *Henry Clay*. Louis says his dad paid Aaron back eventually.

Louis, like many of his relatives, was an oysterman. He started at his trade when he was just eight years old, working during summers and on weekends during World War II. At that time, his dad moved from Foster's Corner to the house across from where Louis and Kit currently live. His father didn't have a car at the time, so Fred would awaken Louis at three in the morning, and they would walk to Matt's Landing Road. Even back then, the railroad was running, and the train came down twice a day. Louis's grandpop would walk out to meet them, and they would walk to the Maurice River and row the boat out to the bay.

It was common practice to buy oysters for seed and put them in the water to mature, so there used to be seed beds up the bay. Oystermen would dredge and catch seed and plant them in the water on ground they leased. Then the oystermen would leave the seed there for five to six years until they grew up. It was a long time to wait, particularly because the oystermen had no way of knowing whether the seed would be eaten by fish, starfish, oyster bores (small snails), or blue claw crabs. As Louis explained, those blue claws can crunch a shell right up. Reportedly, in current times, oystermen planting seed in cages off the bottom of the bay can raise three-inch oysters in a year.

The *Tommy*

At some point, prior to the *Henry Clay*, Fred bought another boat from his brother Aaron called the *Tommy*. She was a twenty-eight-foot-long scow, which is a flat-bottomed boat. Louis used to steer that boat down the creek to East Point and "crab the cove." Louis laughingly remarked that he disliked the *Tommy*, which he described as an inboard boat with a model-A engine in it. The boat had a transmission and clutch and was a direct drive, but the gear shift was sawed off. Louis had to lift the lid off the engine box and put it in gear; he still remembers how doing so would tickle his hand. When his dad would cast off by pushing the boat away from the dock, Louis would have to rip it in gear, then run back to the tiller. The rudderstock was rounded from use, which would cause the prop wash to loosen up and the tiller to come off. When this happened, it rubbed Louis's knuckles raw—particularly in the winter, when his fingers were numb. The 1950 storm eventually destroyed the *Tommy*.

When oystermen discovered oysters in Dennis Creek, a man named Tony D'Agastino became a supplier for what at the time was Fuller's Fish Market in New York, which would buy his oysters in large quantities. Eventually, Louis's family turned the *Tommy* into a houseboat. The family would come down for a week at a time to catch oysters; they'd sell these to Tony, who would sell them to Fuller's. This was during the oyster industry's heyday. Later, when oysters grew scarce because of overharvesting, the "tongers"—another name for oystermen—started cheating the oyster market business. They would put oysters in with empty shells attached or undersized oysters to increase the weight but not the actual harvest. This eventually caused Tony to lose his market and to go out of business.

Problems for the Oysters

Sometime in the 1950s, some people from down on the Cape Shore decided they didn't want oystermen to work Dennis Creek. They put a stop to individual oystermen in that area, and that's the way it still is today.

At some point, the oysters got something called MSX. In Louis's opinion, Haskins, the professor in charge of research on Cape Shore, should have been hanged for what his researchers did down there—apparently, they only monitored the water-pollution situation and took samples but did nothing to correct the problem. There was a dump site off Atlantic City in what was called the bight, where Interstate Oil brought and dumped Philadelphia trash, chemicals, and other debris. Louis knew two captains who worked for that company. They told him strings of barges would take out garbage and other substances and dump them in the Delaware Bay. If the water was rough, they wouldn't go all the way to the dump site; instead, they would dump at the mouth of the bay. When the oysters started getting MSX, people didn't seem to know what it was. They couldn't figure out why oysters and mussels had started dying in Cape May and up the bay. Per Louis, when Interstate Oil was made to stop dumping, an interesting thing happened: the oysters stopped dying.

Tales from Vic Ballato, Former Thompson's Beach Resident

● ● ●

Paradise for the Working Man

Victor Ballato, who owns South Jersey Trucks in Port Elizabeth, New Jersey, was more than happy to reminisce about his time at what he called "the last frontier." Victor and his wife, Jeanette, purchased a vacation home at Thompson's Beach in 1975. Until then, they'd lived year-round in Turnersville, New Jersey, but they were looking for a place by the water.

They drove around and found a home that had been sitting empty for years at Thompson's Beach. They inquired about it locally and found the house's owner, Eleanor Adams. They purchased the home from Eleanor, who'd purchased it from Walt Stowman, the owner of Stowman's Shipyard in nearby Dorchester, New Jersey. The house's builder had been one of the original Thompsons for whom the beach had been named; he had used it as a vacation home. People from town, including one of the local judges, had places at the beach as well. Thompson's Beach was a recreational place like the other shore points of New Jersey, and it drew people looking to enjoy the cool bay breezes in a time before air-conditioning.

One unique aspect of this beach community was that it consisted of mostly middle-class folks who wouldn't otherwise have been able to afford beachfront property. Vic called it "a paradise for the working man."

Friendly Neighbors
Vic and his family fondly remembered many neighbors. Some of his neighbors from the 1970s and 1980s were the Shaws, Krupas, Rumbolds, Robins, Scotts, and Secrests. The summer residents at Thompson's Beach peacefully coexisted. They would look out for one another and greet each other as they strolled along the peaceful beaches.

Star and Dan
Victor shared a few of his favorite memories from his time on Thompson's Beach. One had to do with his dog, Star, who intuitively knew when the bus dropped Victor's kids off down the road after school each day. Star would start to get excited and wag his tail, and he'd want to bound out of the house to greet Rocco and Michael.

Another dog, Dan, became their pet because Dan's former owner couldn't control the dog's incessant barking. Interestingly enough, once this big and rather unintelligent dog arrived at Thompson's Beach, his barking was never again a problem. He played, ran, and sunbathed on the beach to entertain himself. Apparently, Dan found the beach to be a relaxing and stress-reducing place.

Big Blue Claw Crabs
Another of Vic's memories involved the blue-crab-filled inlet across the road behind his house. The crabs were so plentiful that people could see them in the banks along the edges of the water. They could often be scooped out with a net. Vic always had a stash of crabs for company, and they couldn't have been any fresher.

Nature and Wildlife
Vic says he knows people complained about the greenhead flies, but once he raised his house onto pilings, he didn't have an issue again. It seems greenheads can't fly higher than five feet in the air. In addition,

Vic remembers there was usually a nice breeze from the water that kept the bugs away. Occasionally, bugs would find their opportunities in land breezes, but Vic learned to adapt—he even had a weather station that kept him apprised of the wind patterns.

Horseshoe crabs came with the territory. They would lay their eggs in June; this provided meals for millions of birds, including plovers. Later, when the salt-hay meadows were flooded by a utility company, many horseshoe crabs became trapped and died when they couldn't get back to the bay. The locals started to call the meadows "the killing fields" afterward.

Turtles are frequently seen at Thompson's Beach and East Point in June each year. They lay their eggs in the sand and by the edges of the roads. The baby turtles march into the bay. (Courtesy of J. Rumbold).

CINDER BLOCKS

It was common in the 1970s for the EP Henry Corporation to bring cinder blocks down to the beach. The blocks only cost five dollars per truckload and served as bulkheads to prevent road erosion. At the time, concrete was not recycled, so it was available as fill and could be used as a protective barrier against the destruction of the road by the bay. Wheaton Glass would also bring truckloads of unusable colored glass, which served as a barricade to the encroaching water. The residents used to refer to these colorful glass beacons as "Thompson's Beach diamonds," and people at surrounding local beaches still find beautiful colored glass on occasion.

SALT-HAY MEADOWS

Vic recalls that the salt-hay industry used to thrive in the area. In fact, the beach was surrounded by salt-hay meadows. The glass companies and other industries once used salt hay to cure concrete. It kept it from cooling down too fast. Today, there are specific covers for this purpose. Businesses also used it as packing material and it was used by farmers for animal fodder and bedding.

This was a typical sight at the height of the salt hay farming industry in the area. These meadows surrounded Thompson's Beach and East Point areas. (Courtesy of Bayshore Center at Bivalve).

UNDOCUMENTED STORM

On October 23, 1980, Thompson's Beach suffered through an undocumented storm—the worst storm Victor remembers from his residency there—caused by a combination of events that created exceptionally high tides. A very high tide wiped out virtually everything, and people in town weren't even aware it was happening. Vic called the local weather bureau to find out why people didn't know about the storm, and employees at the bureau told him the weather bureau was aware of the storm. They encouraged him to get a book from the library that showed the dates of predicted high tides. After the storm, Vic's house was severely damaged, and he had to rebuild it.

Over time, the state bought out the owners who remained in the area, sparking an ongoing battle late in the 1990s. As Vic tells the story, Public Service Electric and Gas (PSE&G) made deals with the salt-hay-meadow landowners, whose properties didn't have much value because they couldn't build on the meadows. Initially, the power company had plans to build a new road and make improvements that pleased the landowners, but the company changed its mind, claiming the proposed changes would leave too big a footprint on the land.

At that time, Thompson's Beach had only a few full-time residents: Vic's family and Leroy Hickman. Even the part-time residents were bitter about what was happening; people did not want to leave.

Memories from Ed Krupa

● ● ●

Duck Hunting

Edward A. Krupa lives in Lawrenceville, New Jersey, now, but he used to own a cottage at Thompson's Beach. As Ed tells it, his time at Thompson's Beach started with duck hunting in the 1960s. Ed, his friends, and relatives kept moving farther south in New Jersey in search of less-crowded places to hunt. His brother-in-law Tommy Wiechnik learned of some places for sale along the bay in Thompson's Beach and bought a place there in the mid-1960s. That place became the family's home away from home and the headquarters for the Thompson's Beach Duck Club.

Working Man's Paradise

When I asked Ed what made Thompson's Beach special, he promptly said it was "the last frontier of New Jersey" —in his opinion, it was a bit like the Wild West, in that nobody knew what was going on or what people were doing there. There weren't a lot of rules. It was a place where one could enjoy simple things and be close to nature. It was a place for family and friends.

In time, Ed bought Tommy's beach home and there was always a lot of traffic at their house with the Krupa kids and their friends. It was a Cape Cod-style home with two bedrooms downstairs and two bedrooms upstairs. Sometimes there would be as many as ten people sleeping on the floor upstairs, so it's not surprising that Ed was always cooking. The family frequently went duck hunting, and when I asked if they ate the ducks,

I learned that the family instead stuffed the animals and used them for décor. He did the taxidermy himself and even showed me a picture of him and his wife standing in front of a wall of stuffed ducks.

According to Ed, fish were plentiful back in the 1960s and 1970s, and former neighbors used to net shad and big weakfish from the beach. The Krupa family used to smoke these catches with an old refrigerator they'd jury-rigged into a smoker. Around this time, they also had an eighteen- to twenty-foot boat named the *Polish Falcon*. They would take the boat out, and if they didn't catch fish in fifteen minutes, they would go back to shore. Ed says the fish are no longer as plentiful.

Eventually, the Krupas bought a different place on the right-hand side of the beach, right on the water. The Krupa home was across the street from a house that once belonged to my grandparents, Wade and Lilian Rumbold, though at the time, the Kardaz family owned it.

Here is a picture of several of the members of the Thompson's Beach Duck Club. (Courtesy of Ed Krupa).

Ed Krupa is seen here cooking in his Thompson's Beach cottage for the weekend visitors who were so much a part of his pleasant memories. (Courtesy of Ed Krupa).

In this photograph, taken in the 1960's, Ed Krupa and his wife, Pat, are standing in front of a wall of trophy ducks accumulated from hunting excursions. (Courtesy of Ed Krupa).

Destroyed by the Storm of 1980

● ● ●

THE KRUPAS OWNED AND ENJOYED the house for about three years before an unnamed storm in 1980 claimed it. When the storm hit, Ed and his children were in the house, while Pat, his wife, was on vacation with a girlfriend in California. Ed and some neighbors had been playing cards and drinking in the evening before he fell asleep. One of his children, Thaddeus, woke Ed when the high water was hitting the front windows of their home. The family had to make a break for it to escape the flooding.

The house across the street from the Krupas' was positioned high off the ground on telephone poles, so Ed and his children hastily climbed the many steps to that house and had to force their way in to safety, as the Kardaz family was out of town. Ed recalls that he paid to replace the window in his neighbors' home after the storm. Ed and his kids watched as strong waves lifted the roof off their house, and it crashed into the water.

Their home was destroyed. It was a frightening time. Ed remembers a couple of men in a boat in the canal behind the Kardazes' house calling to him and his children, attempting a rescue. By this point, it was a little late, however; the water had already receded, and the high waters and strong winds had subsided. Ed and the children walked to safety.

Tribute to Dick Secrest

● ● ●

THE POLISH ARMY

THE FOLLOWING MEMORIES ARE FROM an e-mail Ed Krupa wrote for his friend Dick Secrest who passed away in 2016. Ed and Dick were friends for fifty-five years. They first met when Ed was the vice president at a family-owned business called White Eagle Publishing. Dick, who owned an electrical contracting company, came in to White Eagle to get a monthly company newsletter published. They became fast friends. Their friendship quickly came to involve duck hunting. The friends kept moving farther south in New Jersey to find less-crowded places to hunt, and their numbers kept expanding to include their children and Ed's brother-in-law Tommy. Dick affectionately called them all, himself included, the "Polish army" because of their heritage.

On one of their hunting trips, Dick lost the motor off his sneak-box hunting boat while driving to Thompson's Beach. They didn't discover that the motor was gone until they arrived at the beach. They retraced their steps and found it lying in the middle of the main road, still fixed to the transom. They had a good laugh over that, especially since there was no damage done to the motor.

Tommy allowed Dick to put a trailer on his property, and the Secrests enjoyed these accommodations for several years. Eventually, Dick built his own A-frame home farther down the beach, high up on pilings and with a beautiful view of the bay. In time, they sold it to a buyer who moved it inland, where it stands today.

CHIEF ENGINEER

The neighbors banded together to put in pilings and fortify the road, so authorities would not make them leave the beach. They spent many days with a neighbor named Leroy Hickman who had a gigantic loader crane. Dick was always able to fix the machine when it broke down, and the community considered him the "chief engineer" on every project they undertook. It didn't matter if the projects was electrical or mechanical—Dick was always the "go-to guy" when Ed, his sons, or other family members needed advice. Time marched on, and Ed and Dick fought local authorities and agencies until the government made residents sell their homes and leave.

The Secrest A-Frame house at Thompson's Beach is the
subject of this photograph. (Courtesy of Ed Krupa).

THE LURE OF THE AREA

The lure of the area kept pulling them together, and they all ended up at the next beach over, a spot on the bay called East Point. Ed ended up there with his rather large trailer, which featured the "Jersey Room," where he and his friends played countless hands of a card game called catch five. The Krupas also hosted the annual Duck Club Trapshooting Tournament each spring, starting in the 1960s at Thompson's Beach and continuing to the present day at East Point, where thirty-plus people eat and socialize for the weekend.

A New Home for the Secrests

After a short time, Dick built a lovely home for his wife, Nita, high up, out of harm's way, and with a bayfront view. Over the years, the Secrests and their friends did a lot of fishing from their pier, and Ed's family launched lots of boats from the Secrest boat launch.

Flag-Raising Ceremony

Dick also left his mark when he instituted daily flag raising at the lighthouse. He, Tommy, and another friend would get together at the lighthouse and raise the American flag each day during the summer for at least a five-year period. This was another demonstration of how Dick was a leader for his friends, neighbors, and family.

Tommy Joseph Wiechnik Tales

● ● ●

It Even Had Toothpicks

I met with Ed Krupa's brother-in-law Tommy Wiechnik on a Saturday in October 2016. Tom, known as Tommy, and his wife, Lyn, were at Ed's East Point place, and the two men began by showing me pictures they had of places at Thompson's Beach.

I asked Tom how he ended up getting his place at the beach. In February 1968, he came down from Trenton with his brother Frank and a friend named Ed Robbins to look at a house for sale at East Point. He didn't like the house, which wasn't in good shape.

As they left East Point, they saw a Thompson's Beach Road sign and decided to see what was there. Tom recalls driving down the road to the entrance of the beach and having to choose between a left or right turn. He chose left and proceeded to where they saw twin Cape Cod—style homes on the bay. The houses had cedar siding, and one was for sale. Tom told his brother, "I am buying that house."

Frank said, "You are nuts. There's nothing here."

But Tom repeated, "I'm buying it." He went to a pay phone and put in a dime to call the owners in Summerville, New Jersey. He met them and bought the house, for which he paid $5,500—quite a deal for a beachfront home. The house was fully furnished with everything needed. There were even toothpicks in the kitchen. When Tom's family got there in 1968, there were about forty-five houses at the beach.

BOOZING AND CRUISING

According to Ed, "the whole experience was about fishing and duck hunting and boozing and cruising (on boats, not cars)." The men came down every weekend, and they couldn't wait to get to the beach. A lot of the time, Pat, Ed's wife, would stay down during the week with the kids while he went home to work. On one such occasion, Ed recalls, the milkman, who still delivered milk in glass bottles to residents' homes, tried to make out with Pat. Fortunately, she did not respond to his advances!

Tommy and Olga Wiecknik owned this trailer which sat next to their cottage at Thompson's Beach. (Courtesy of Tommy Wiecknik).

Tommy Wiecknik and Ed Krupa are seen here with family members playing a card game at Thompson's Beach. (Courtesy of Tommy Wiecknik).

Rental Agreement—One Case of Beer per Year

As Tom recalls, in the late 1960s, Dick Secrest rented a trailer on the Wiechnik's bayfront property at Thompson's Beach from him. Tom told me the rental agreement simply consisted of one case of beer per year, payable to Tom.

Ed and Tom have many fond memories of people staying at the cottage on the weekends, and Tom moved to the beach full-time in 1978 when he got a job as a guard at the local prison. Tom's family moved to Heislerville after the 1980 storm.

Speakeasy Raid

Tom also remembers a time he and Olga, his wife at the time, were going to meet my parents, Ron and Maura Rumbold, at Captain Badger's Speakeasy at East Point Beach. The speakeasy was a popular place because it was a dry township where alcohol could not be sold. Badger's had been at East Point for decades, and many local people would gather there on the weekends to eat, drink, dance, and play pool. Since Thompson's Beach and East Point were adjacent to each other and joined by a long stretch of beach, Tom and Olga decided to walk up the beach to get there instead of driving. My parents, who drove, were there a couple of hours before them. When Tom and Olga approached Badger's on foot, they saw flashing lights and lots of police cars. They turned right around and headed back to Thompson's Beach. My parents were among many people arrested in an Alcoholic Beverage Control raid that day.

Succession of a Home

As we reminisced about East Point stories and people who lived there at the time, Tom discussed Bill Ferrell, a union guy he liked who used to live at East Point. Apparently, James Jackson, a long-term resident at East Point Beach, sold his house to Bill Ferrell, who sold it to Dick Secrest. The Secrest house still stands at East Point Beach.

Coast Guard Rescue

Once, when Tom and two of his friends were in a low sneak-box hunting boat, they chose to fish in a spot off the turn buoys in the bay out from East Point. They were catching weakfish, and the seas were very calm. The coast guard spotted the men and thought their boat had sunk—apparently, it looked to them as though Tom and his friends were sitting on a log in the water. The coast guard rushed to rescue the men, but when they came up next to the boat, they could see the men weren't in trouble. Everyone had a good laugh, and Tom and his friends caught a lot of weakies (a term for weakfish) that day. In fact, Tom jokes that people can blame former Thompson's Beach residents for the lack of fish left in the sea.

A Partying Place

Tom and Ed also remember all the parties that took place at Thompson's Beach through the decades. There were a lot of parties between Friday and Sunday nights. There was even drinking connected to political campaigns in our dry county.

At one point, in about 1976, the Thompson's Beach Civic Association wanted Tom to run for president. His next-door neighbor at the time, Bert, said she would be his campaign manager. It took Bert and Tom two days to go the full length of the beach while campaigning, because everyone invited them in to drink. They were shot after that first day and couldn't get it all done in one weekend. Eventually, the townspeople voted Tom in as president. His secretary was Bernice Myers. Tom says the association accomplished a lot of work with the township, including roadwork, during his term.

The War Was Lost

A long-term battle between the beach residents, the township, and the state ensued in the 1980s and 1990s. A group of beach residents paid for a lawyer to represent them at a meeting with top people from the New Jersey Department of Environmental Protection (DEP), but Ed Krupa presented the case. Pictures were presented by the DEP that had been taken at a high tide and during a full moon, when there was significant flooding. The residents fought their battles but lost the war, and all home owners were eventually made to leave Thompson's Beach.

Tom had his cottage at Thompson's Beach from 1968 until August 1997, when the township, state, and owners of the nuclear-power plant forced all the residents to leave. He claims these entities were in cahoots with one another. The government forced residents to leave because of the township's resolution of condemnation. The township and state purchased their homes, which were torn down in 1998.

This is a view of Thompson's Beach looking west from the Wiecknik home. (Courtesy of Tommy Wiecknik).

The Myer's home was right on the bay at Thompson's Beach. (Courtesy of Tommy Wiecknik).

A Maurice River Township (MRT) Memory

● ● ●

A Local Legend

Local resident Bill Hawn first shared this story with the Maurice River Township Heritage Society, but he gave me permission to share his memories in this book as well. His story resonates with me because the subject of this story was well-known in the area; in fact, Bob Harris helped to move the cottage my parents purchased out of the salt-hay meadow.

Here's Bill's story, in his own words:

To those of us of a certain age, the sound was as familiar as the DDT sprayer coming down the road on a summer evening, signaling time for a bike ride, the rattle of sand trucks crossing the bridge in the distance on a still winter day, or the smell of Suzy Bel in the late summer or early fall. To me it was the sound of a marvel of engineering headed my way...the rumble of Bob Harris on his tractor coming down the road. I will reflect on the man himself another time; right now, the miracle of his machine is the memory. It always reminded me of contraptions in Rube Goldberg cartoons and would have fit right into a Mad Max movie. The mechanics of it always fascinated me, from the positions of the boom, the way the cable was weaved through pulleys back to the winch, to the way he seemingly had more tools on the thing then was possible. He always seemed to have the spare part or tool that was needed to complete the job.

Bob drove several wells for my father, so I got to see the operation up close; to this day, I barely understand its working. Crafted from an old duel wheel truck (I'm assuming here), the thing was welded and cobbled together from pieces of pipe and parts from God only knows what other machinery. Clutches, spindles, brakes, pulleys, gears, chains, and cables all hooked together made the thing work. I know firsthand that some parts and pieces were held in place with baling wire and twine. Over time, different accessories (smile) were added, from half a windshield, to a keg for the gas tank, and I'm sure the seat was changed out from time to time. A steel footlocker welded on the front for storage and several coffee cans stashed here and there were the only protection from rain and snow that I know of. I never remember seeing a cover over the engine, leaving it open to the weather during every season. Looking back, that impresses me most because it always started (sometimes coaxed by Bob with some unsavory words), but it started nonetheless. Imagine trying that with an auto of today. The versatility of the thing also always fascinated me. I've seen the rig drive wells, pull stumps, haul railroad ties, and load scrap, but with the right angle on the boom and the deft hands its wizened operator running the winch, I never remember it failing to complete the task at hand. In today's world, the thing would never be allowed on the road, and I am sure several safety regulations would be violated with every use of the boom and winches. But the chugga chugga of its motor and the cackle of its driver coming down the road are a part of my MRT heritage that will never be duplicated and a memory I will never forget.

TERROR ON THE BAY

When Tina was eighteen years old and eight months pregnant, she went out in a small rental boat with Pop Pop. (He'd sold the *Lilian* by this time.) When they started out, the sky was clear, and the bay was calm. Pop Pop and Tina weren't planning a long fishing excursion, but they found a good spot and started catching weakfish and flounder. They were a good distance from shore when the sky got cloudy, and a storm blew up suddenly. They prepared to head back to dock, but the rain started with a vengeance, and visibility became poor. The water got rough, and Tina and Pop Pop lost their way.

Tina thought she, Pop Pop, and her unborn baby were going to die. She says she had never been so frightened in her life. She knew she wouldn't be able to swim the distance back to shore if the boat capsized, and they wouldn't survive. Yet she always had blind trust in Pop Pop. They made it back, and my nephew Ronnie is now a grown man.

Christina Longley fondly recalled favorite Thompson's Beach Memories in a word picture which is here illustrated by my son and artist, Adam Valenzano. (Courtesy of Christina Longley and Adam Valenzano).

ARRIVAL OF A MOVIE STAR

My sister and I both remember the day a movie star arrived at our family pier in a big yacht. Readers born in the 1940s or 1950s and from the Philadelphia area may remember Sally Starr, who had a show for children that we used to watch faithfully. Sally would always dress as a cowgirl with a beautiful sequined satin blouse and a wonderful fancy cowgirl hat. Well, that day, Tina and I were at the end of the pier checking crab pots when, lo and behold, a huge boat pulled up. There Sally stood, in full regalia.

Apparently, Sally and her captain were lost on their way to an appearance in Atlantic City. Tina and I ran to get our parents, loudly saying Sally Starr was there. At first, our parents doubted us; after all, it wasn't every day that a movie star showed up at Thompson's Beach. It didn't take long, however, for them to spot an especially large yacht docked at our pier. What an unexpected and exciting event for an otherwise routine day at the beach!

Lilian, Ronald and Julie Rumbold are posing on the front porch of Wade and Lilian's cottage at Thompson's Beach. This was taken in the summer of 1964. (Courtesy of the Rumbold collection).

In this photograph are Linda Laxton with Wade Rumbold, Ronald and Christina Rumbold, Frank Laxton and Julie Rumbold in Wade and Lilian's cottage at Thompson's Beach. (Courtesy of J. Rumbold collection).

Chick Foster's Recollections

● ● ●

Washed through the Meadows

Charles (Chick) Foster and his sister, Sharon Johnson, were born and raised in in the town of Leesburg, which is in close proximity to Thompson's Beach. Karen Lee, another local resident, asked the siblings to share with me some of their childhood and growing-up memories of the local beaches. Chick wanted to make sure I knew that a lot of the small homes along Glade and East Point Roads in Heislerville had been washed there through the meadows from Thompson's Beach and East Point after numerous bad storms over the years.

Hunting Times

Some of Chick's earliest and fondest memories are of hunting with his dad (who was also nicknamed Chick) at Thompson's Beach in the 1960s. They would traipse through the meadows in their boots and hunting clothes with their shotguns slung over their shoulders. He says there were plentiful pheasants and ducks at the time. It was a popular hunting spot frequented by many of the local people.

Teenage Muscle at the Beach

When Chick got to be a teenager, he would drive down to the beach. All the kids would park their big, fast muscle cars at the bulkhead by the water and drink beer. Everyone would have the radios cranking their favorite music. It was a great place to socialize, and the police didn't bother the kids back in those times: they weren't doing any harm, and it was a safe place, out of the way, for them to hang out by the water.

Lots of Rowboats

Sharon and Chick's dad always had a boat back then, which he would keep in their yard. There used to be a dock at the end of their street that all the neighbors could use to put their boats in the water. They didn't have to pay to use it; it was just a handshake deal in that the person who owned the dock agreed to let the local people launch their boats there and never asked for money. Chick and his dad used to go out in the bay and catch weakfish. They would fill coolers and have so many fish that they would give them away. Chick says Brooks Rumbold, my great-uncle, would also give fish to the neighbors, because he was quite an active fisherman at the time. According to Chick, most people in the area at the time had garveys or rowboats and fished and crabbed locally.

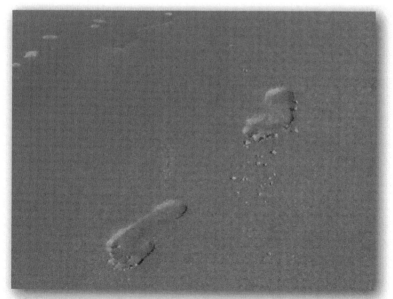

Year after year, the residents of and visitors to Thompson's Beach and East Point left their footprints in the sand. (Courtesy of Ronald Flynn).

Karen Lee Stories

• • •

Finding Treasure

KAREN LEE LIVED IN PORT Elizabeth, New Jersey, as a child and currently lives in nearby Leesburg. She remembers coming to East Point as a kid and collecting slag glass in beautiful colors. Her family would take chunks home and make glass rock gardens with flowers in between the lovely glass pieces. Her sister owns the homestead with the rock gardens now and takes very good care of them. Karen says spotting slag glass was like finding treasure, especially when the sun shone on the glass, and it sparkled. Karen still occasionally finds pieces of glass shining in the sun, and she says other people come looking for it even now. In 2016, down at Thompson's Beach, she found one big piece of glass, but she mostly finds many small pieces these days.

Teenage Memories

As a teenager, Karen would come down to Thompson's Beach in the evenings with her boyfriend, Gary. Gary and Karen would hang out with Linda Laxton and Donna Johnson, who were cousins and summer residents at Thompson's Beach, and make bonfires on the beach. Some of these teenagers who met at the beach later ended up marrying each other. In fact, Karen and Gary ended up in a long and happy marriage.

One of the things Karen and Gary liked to do back then—which Karen still does to this day—is take a metal detector to East Point and Thompson's Beach. She says they've found jewelry and at least one ring per search over the years, as well as many silver coins. One of her favorite finds was a silver ring in an antique setting.

Visiting the Past with Skip DeGlavina

• • •

A Sailor and a City Girl

In fall 2016, I met with Skip DeGlavina at Chick Foster's house in Leesburg, New Jersey. Skip grew up in Leesburg after his family moved there in 1943. His parents were immigrants; his dad was from Italy, and his mom was from Hungary. Skip's father was a merchant seaman; when the war started, naturally, he was at sea. When his ship was sunk, he decided he didn't want to do that again, and he bought a chicken farm in Leesburg. Skip's mom was a city girl from New York, and Skip's parents met in the city and got married— imagine a sailor and a city girl getting married and moving to rural South Jersey. Skip's father found the place because he had merchant-seamen friends who lived in Vineland, New Jersey, and he got to know the area as a result.

Skip's parents' house was one of the only ones with indoor plumbing back then, as his mother refused to move to a place with an outhouse. My sister, Tina, and Skip both remember that there were many outhouses in the 1940s. In fact, our great-grandfather's home in Leesburg, where our grandmother grew up, had an outhouse.

Skip grew up on the farm and learned at a young age to help with the livestock. There were no days off, as animals needed to be fed and cared for regardless of the day of the week. Skip says this taught him responsibility at an early age.

Hangout Area

When I asked Skip if he had any Thompson's Beach memories, he laughed and said, "Oh yeah!" According to Skip, Thompson's Beach was a hangout area, where kids did normal growing-up sorts of things like gathering in groups and listening to music; teenagers from Leesburg used to go there to party and have fun. Skip spent most of his time there in his late teens and early twenties, mostly in the late 1960s. The beach was a community back then, with lots of houses and families, and Skip and his friends used to go fishing and crabbing down there. He remembers Russ's Rentals and says Thompson's Beach was a thriving community even when he was a young child. He used to go swimming with his parents at a nice beach right near the main entrance to Thompson's Beach.

Badger's as a Talking Point

Skip says his friends all tried to get into Captain Badger's Speakeasy at one time or another. Betty Archie, another local resident who was with us as we talked, says she never tried to get in, because she was a good girl. Badger's was always a talking point for the locals in the 1960s, though the lighthouse was a great spot to park and hang out as well—East Point was one of the better parking spots, as it was rather remote.

This photograph was taken in the decades before the fire of 1971 which destroyed a good portion of the lighthouse roof. (Courtesy of Mary Hagemann).

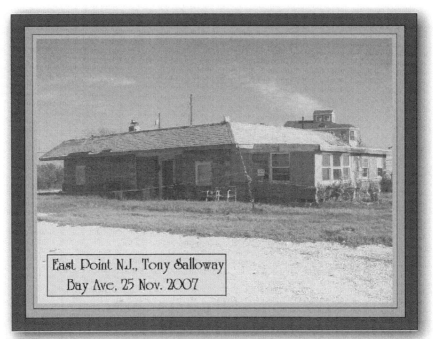

East Point N.J., Tony Salloway
Bay Ave, 25 Nov. 2007

This building once belonged to Captain Harry Badger and was the site of the infamous Badger's Speakeasy. In 2007, it was owned by Tony Salloway. The building has since been torn down. (Courtesy of Richard St. Aubyn

BEING A KID BY THE RIVER

The Leesburg kids did what kids do used to do in the 1950s and 1960s, like ride bicycles and play ball, except that they were fortunate enough to have a river in their backyards. They would hang out at the Maurice River in Leesburg during the warm summer months. At the time, people could put boats in the river without having to pay.

One of Skip's best friends had a lot to do with the Delaware Bay Shipbuilding Company, in Leesburg, especially during the war years. Skip got to spend a lot of time there as a child, because the shipyard was right down the street from where he grew up. He remembers diving off and swimming around the oyster boats that were docked there. Just about every kid had some sort of boat, and Skip was no exception; he had a little eight-foot rowboat. Somehow, he and his friends found a three-horse motor for the little boat, and he could make it fly. Skip and his friends knew every cove in the river. They also would put in inner tubes and swim with the tide to Stowman's Wharf in Dorchester, a distance of probably two or three miles. It was a good time to be growing up.

Skip vaguely remembers "the Flood," which is how many people refer to the storm of 1950. He remembers going down to Thompson's Beach with his parents and seeing houses floating in the meadows. He knew people had lost their lives, but he was young and doesn't remember much else about it.

Skip says that fifty years ago, there were probably an additional two to three hundred feet of land just to get to the beach at East Point. Now, the water is nearly right up to the lighthouse, as the area has seen a lot of erosion in the past several decades.

An Oysterman during Prohibition

The father of one of Skip's best friends growing up was an oysterman during Prohibition. According to Skip, most of the oystermen back in those days never went more than about twelve miles from Leesburg. Yet this man went all the way to Cuba and picked up rum. While sailing back, he got as far as Charleston, South Carolina, before he ran into bad weather. The crew, concerned about getting caught, bailed on him. Amazingly, he sailed that boat back to Leesburg by himself. When he got home, he stored the booze in their farmhouse attic and slowly dispersed it. Talk about an adventurer!

My Stories

• • •

BOTH RUMBOLDS

IN 1963, MY DAD, RONALD Rumbold, hired some locals to move the cottage he and my mom purchased for $150. (No, I am not kidding.) The house had floated away, and it and was in the salt-hay meadow behind Thompson's Beach because of a storm in 1962.

I was just seven years old at the time, but I have vague memories of the moving of the house. It was one of the highlights of the summer. An old farmer, Bob Harris, used his tractor and massive ropes to roll the small house on telephone poles through the meadow and onto solid ground. From there they placed it on pilings that had been sunk deep into the ground to elevate the house and keep it safe from future flooding. Friends, family, and other locals assisted with the daunting task of saving a house to make a home.

I am sure it took quite a lot of effort and sweat to safely transport a house over tall reeds, uneven ground, and lots of mud, but in the pictures, the guys look like they might have been enjoying themselves somewhat. I guess the whole male hunter-gatherer thing might have been a factor. They may not have been hunting ducks or deer, but they captured and secured a house.

The part I recall from when I was a young, impressionable child was when the workers were moving the house and securing it onto pilings. One of the large ropes suddenly snapped and flung through the air, catching the back of my grandfather Wade Rumbold's neck. The rope pulled a large layer of skin right off below his hairline, but it could have been much worse. He required first aid but was all right.

This small group of persistent men accomplished their goal, and the house was placed next to our grandparents' house. Eventually, by the later 1960s, we placed a sign that read BOTH RUMBOLDS between the two cottages. Looking back on it now, I realize how truly blessed we were to have beachfront property next to our grandparents.

Sea Glass

• • •

ONE OF MY FAVORITE MEMORIES is how the sea glass by the beach would sparkle in the sun. In the 1960s and 1970s, Wheaton Glass, then a thriving enterprise in Millville, New Jersey, would donate its extra or unusable slag glass. Individuals and the township would bring the glass down in a dump truck to Thompson's Beach and place it along the gravel road on the bay side as a barricade against the encroaching water.

At times, the glass would be piled four to five feet high. These mounds consisted of concrete, rock, and large chunks of colorful glass. As I recall, the colors included turquoise, purple, green, brown, milk-glass white, and clear. Over time, the bay would polish and smooth out the sharp edges of the glass. When we experienced storms or high winds with extreme tides during full or new moons, the barricades would wash away. Later, residents and visitors would find pieces of slag glass shimmering along the beach or sparkling in the sunlight. It was like finding treasure.

In the early days, there were large chunks, sometimes twelve inches or more in diameter. I loved finding the purple ones, though turquoise was my second favorite. Neighbors had collections of what we called sea glass or "Thompson's Beach diamonds," and many former residents still have collections they've transported to their current homes.

Here are cousins, Julie and Ellen Rumbold, in the surf at Thompson's Beach in the early 1960's. (Courtesy of the Rumbold collection).

In this photograph are summer friends, Julie Rumbold, Donna and Kenny Johnson, and Linda Laxton. We were frequently playing in the bay. (Courtesy of Julie Rumbold).

"Murder" at Thompson's Beach

● ● ●

MY SISTER, TINA, WAS ABOUT fifteen years old at the time of this terrifying event, and I was eight. We were at the Thompson's Beach cottage alone, as our parents were at Captain Badger's, a speakeasy at East Point Beach, at the time. (Though *speakeasy* is a term from the Prohibition era, this was around 1964.)

It would have been late afternoon or early evening; it was daylight, nonetheless. Tina and I were inside the cottage when we heard loud voices outside. We looked out the front windows and saw a neighbor woman chasing her husband with a large kitchen knife. They were headed toward our cottage! Tina and I quickly locked the front door and pulled down the forest-green window shades. We peeked around the edges of the shades to see what was happening. When we did, we saw the man with the knife in his hand. He jabbed it into the wooden edge of our front deck, and we saw his wife lying motionless in the sand in front of our house.

Needless to say, our young minds jumped immediately to the conclusion that this man had gotten the knife from his wife and killed her! We immediately used the phone to call our parents at Captain Badger's. Our frightened call got their attention quickly. Our folks left East Point immediately to return with a posse of their friends and neighbors. When Tina and I looked out the windows again, the man was carrying the woman back toward their cottage. We thought he was taking her lifeless body back to dispose of the evidence. After all, we were surrounded by water, which would be a convenient place to dispose of a murder victim.

Once the "rescue team" arrived from East Point, we learned the true facts of the situation. The man's wife had been drinking excessively. In a drunken rage, she had chased her husband with the knife. He wrestled the weapon away, and she passed out drunk on the sand in front of our cottage. Then he carried her back to their home. What a relief!

The Days of Baby Oil and Iodine

● ● ●

FOR US, THEY WEREN'T THE "Days of Wine and Roses," as Jack Lemmon experienced in a 1962 film of the same name; they were the days of baby oil and iodine (and beer and crab picking). The days of baby oil and iodine were "the good old days," when we didn't have a care in the world—the days of youth, when summers lingered. It was also a time when sunbathing was quite the thing to do.

That's right. It was the time before anyone knew how bad it was to lie in the sun and bake. It was the time when everyone wanted skin as dark as it could get. We would mix iodine and baby oil, rub the resulting substance on our bodies, and almost literally fry in the sun. Oh, it looked good in our younger days—not so much now, with wrinkles and skin cancer! My aunt Christina, my mother's sister, had more money than we did, so she would bring Bain de Soleil tanning oil down to the beach when she visited. She looked so glamorous wearing her bikinis and sunglasses, lying on the beach, and getting her tan.

The kids and adults would all lie out on the beach or the pier, getting as much color as they could with whatever melanin their bodies could produce and using whatever tools were at their disposal. People then definitely got healthy doses of vitamin D as well.

Thompson's Beach residents, Julie Rumbold, Jackie King and Toddy Lee are enjoying a ride at Thompson's beach in the back of an old pick-up truck in the early 1960's. (Courtesy of Ronald and Maura Rumbold collection).

Bunch of Girls at the Beach

● ● ●

THE SUMMER AFTER I GRADUATED from eighth grade at Our Lady of Charity Catholic School in Brookhaven, Pennsylvania, my mom and dad let me bring down a truck full of girls for a weekend at the beach. This was also in the days when parents let children ride in the backs of pickup trucks, in the open air, with no seat belts and no apparent concerns for safety. (How did any of us survive without seat belts?) We never knew until that weekend that there were so many boys in the Heislerville and Leesburg vicinity—big mistake on my parents' part! Once the girls arrived, put on their swimsuits, went out to the beach, and slathered on the oil, the boys seemed to come out of the woodwork. It was a rough weekend for my parents and a fun weekend for a group of fourteen-year-old girls. I was never allowed to bring a bunch of girls to the beach again. My parents liked to drink…maybe it started in earnest that weekend.

A Head Start on Driving

● ● ●

I MAY NOT HAVE GOTTEN a driver's license until I was sixteen years of age, but I was driving when I was nine years old. My dad would let me sit on his lap and steer whatever big American automobile we had at the time. I looked forward to these times I spent with my father, learning to steer a car. He loved cars; consequently, we had a variety of them over the years. They were typically the kind of big-block Chevys and Fords people like to collect and take to car shows these days. When I grew tall enough for my feet to reach the pedals, Dad taught me to drive a Ford Galaxy 500. By the time I was old enough to get a permit, I was very comfortable behind the wheel.

The father of a friend at the beach, Linda Laxton, owned an automotive-repair shop in Chester, Pennsylvania. Somehow, he came across a miniature antique car, which he brought to the beach for Linda and her brother, Larry, to tool around in. Linda would let me drive the car, which was probably only about five feet long and four feet wide, as well. We had a good time.

Tina remembers driving our grandfather's old Ford truck when she was just a child. It must have been a tradition at the beach to develop young drivers. Tina remembers a hair-raising event that happened late at night when she was about thirteen years old—I would have been six at the time. We were at our cottage with our mom, Maura, at the time, while Dad was back in Pennsylvania working at Sun Oil. At around two o'clock in the morning, the three of us were awakened by the sounds of cars and whooping and hollering young men outside our home. When we got up and peeked from behind the blinds, we saw at least three cars wildly circling both Rumbolds' cottages. If we had been wagon trains, it would have been like being surrounded by Native Americans. Tina says it was the scariest thing she remembers. Mom called the state police, but the hoodlums were gone by the time they arrived. It was probably just a bunch of drunken teenagers out carousing. Maybe someone reading this book may know who these characters were!

Thompson's Beach Picnic

● ● ●

My husband, John, is a romantic at heart. So when he suggested we have a picnic by the water at Thompson's Beach in summer 2014, I gladly agreed. John knew how much I loved the place, and he had heard many of my childhood beach stories. My husband is a car collector, and he happened to be driving the H1 Humvee on this particular sunny August day. We knew the truck would get through just about anything, and we discovered the unlocked gate at the entrance of the rough, rocky access leading to the beach.

John; our beloved golden retriever, Sarah Paws; and I drove over the rocky road and parked near the sand. We had a delicious feast of fried chicken and biscuits while we savored the view of the bay and enjoyed the warm sunshine and gentle breeze.

East Point Stories

• • •

The East Point Hotel

Louis Peterson learned from Roland Butcher, a local man who owned a lot of land in and around Thompson's Beach many years ago, that the hotel at East Point was built on sacred Native American ground sometime in the mid-1800s. The Lenni-Lenape Indians used to summer in the East Point area, because it was cooler for them by the water, and they could catch fish. Reportedly, when workers were digging the hotel's foundation, they discovered intact human skeletons that were seven feet tall.

According to Louis, the large wooden hotel was built in the first place because boats coming from Philadelphia to Cape May were not able to "carry the tide" the full distance. This means the tide was too low at points for the boats to continue their journey south, so they needed a place where they could anchor the boats, go ashore around East Point, and wait to catch the tide the next day. It was convenient for them to have an overnight layover at the hotel. The next day, they would catch what sailors called the "fair tide," a current that increases a boat's speed, the rest of the way to Cape May. Back in the late 1800s, the boats were sailing vessels, so these tides were very important to their journeys.

East Point House

There seems to be some discrepancy about the name of the large wooden hotel that graced East Point in the 1800s. When I spoke with East Point

Beach resident Richard "Saint" St. Aubyn, he told me he knows it as the Zane Hotel. As far as Saint knows, someone named Zane owned the hotel. On a map from the late 1800s, however, the building is listed as the East Point House.

Saint and his son Rick heard the hotel had a bowling alley and a large stable that held many horses. They also heard there was a time when hundreds of residents lived at East Point.

A MYSTERIOUS STAIN ON THE ATTIC FLOOR OF THE EAST POINT LIGHTHOUSE

According to Louis Peterson, the stain on the lighthouse's attic floor "was dark, almost black but not black, irregular in shape and about eighteen to twenty-four inches around. At that time, before the fire destroyed it, access to the lantern room was through a door in the north side of the eastern half of the attic, then up a short stairway on the left that connected the attic floor to a landing under the lantern room. A short ladder then extended from the platform to a hinged trapdoor that was the actual entrance into the lantern room itself. Under this stairway and platform was a closet accessed through a door in the western half of the attic. The stain was a short distance outside this door toward the window."

Louis says he "always thought somebody in the past had spilled oil or something there. Years later, as a married man with children, I spoke with Roland Butcher, then an old man who was born and raised in Heislerville, and the stain entered the conversation. He said it was blood. The way he told it was that during Prohibition, a person he didn't name had a short-wave radio set up in the closet and was using it to direct rum runners around coast guard patrol boats. The coast guard raided the lighthouse and shot and killed him there."

Louis has never found any documents to support this tale. True or not, he doesn't know, but the story is interesting anyhow, as government records of the lighthouse are incomplete for this period.

EAST POINT LIGHTHOUSE RECOLLECTIONS FROM AN OYSTERMAN

Per Louis, Joshua Brick, a local man of prominence in the 1800s, was responsible for getting the lighthouse built. Louis believes Joshua ramrodded that lighthouse through the regulatory approval process and eventually sold the land to the government. Louis's dad and grand-pop moved into the lighthouse in 1920, because his grandfather, Aaron, was the lighthouse's custodian from 1920 to 1923. He was paid one dollar per year. Louis's father was thirteen years old when they moved there.

EAST POINT LIGHTHOUSE PROHIBITION STORY

Karen Lee shared this story from the 1930s with me, though she wasn't comfortable sharing names, because at least one of the people in the story is still alive. According to Karen, it was a pitch-dark night, and the moon was covered by clouds.

That night a box truck sat parked by the lighthouse, waiting for a shipment of booze to come in from the water by boat. The truck would then distribute the rum inland. The truck's driver didn't know, however, that there had been a raid, and the shipment was not destined to arrive. Some local people, involved with the rum-running trade, found out and sent a man and his eleven-year-old son as messengers to let the truck driver know he should leave.

When the man and his son got to the truck, they didn't see any signs of the truck driver. They cautiously approached and knocked on the driver's-side window. Much to their surprise, the driver, who had been sleeping, popped up with a tommy gun in his hands! (According to my husband, a class-III gun dealer, gangsters used this style of machine gun in the 1930s.) As the story goes, the truck driver did not fire the gun, and the father and son lived to tell the story for many years. In fact, per Karen, even when the son was eighty-six years old, he was still telling the tale!

In those days, oyster boats were very prevalent. According to Karen, many of the oystermen made their money during Prohibition and were able to afford their boats because of rum-running.

Joseph Peacock Boat Rentals at East Point Lighthouse

Captain Joseph Peacock was the lighthouse's custodian from 1926 to 1938. The Lighthouse Service paid keepers only a dollar a year to maintain the lighthouse; in exchange, they were able to live in the lighthouse free of charge. Reportedly, Joseph obtained permission to build and operate a boat-rental place at the lighthouse while he was there. For that reason, he remained probably the longest of any of the custodians. Apparently, it was a successful business, with more than twenty boats for rent. Joseph also had food for purchase there, and he sold the operation to the custodian who followed him. Each succeeding custodian purchased the business.

East Point Civic Association

Richard St. Aubyn gave me an old 1970's dark brown naugahyde briefcase. Its contents were unbeknownst to me. He told me it contained information from the East Point Civic Association. Discovering the items in the briefcase was an adventure in and of itself. These handwritten documents displayed to me the dedication of the former residents for the preservation of East Point Beach and their love for the place they called home.

Interestingly, I also discovered drugs in the briefcase. Fortunately, they were just Tylenol Sinus tablets. The expiration date was 1976!

The remainder of the contents were mostly minutes from many meetings over the years from 1957 when the East Point Civic Association was founded until 1996 when the meeting minutes seemed to end. Two of the founders were Ed and Mary Britty. The initial minutes stated that the object of the association was to improve living conditions at East Point and create better fellowship. Members were defined as persons who paid their full assessment as agreed by membership. The annual fee was ten dollars per year.

There were two pictures of Mary and one of Ed Britty and an unknown neighbor dated 1958. Some of the names from the late 1950's included Mr. and Mrs. Henry, Gus Varadi, Helen and Arthur Russetto, Mr. and Mrs. Antanavich, Mrs. B. A. Breeden, Mr. and Mrs. W. E. Hinch, Ester and Frank Noya, Carl Johnson and William Duvall, Mr. and Mrs. John Marlin, Mr. and Mrs. Harry Sturgis and James Jackson.

Mr. Jackson was the first elected President of the Association. The initial meetings were mostly about dues, having a well put in and about township maintenance of the beach road. The mimeographed and hand written lined paper smelled old and was fun to read. The penmanship was mostly beautiful, old fashioned writing.

There were some names from the 1960's that I recognized. Among them were Jimmy Buckley, Harry Badger and Dolly Laxton. Mrs. Frank Laxton was a Thompson's Beach resident. There was a short time, which was probably just a few years, when East Point and Thompson's Beach residents combined efforts to preserve and save the beaches. Exploring the contents of this briefcase was a blast from the past.

Most of the business items had to do with drinking water. How to get it, how to pay for a well, a pump and pipes, how to keep it clean for drinking purposes, who was paying for their access and who wasn't. There was also discussion of road repairs by the township after flooding and ongoing need for road replacement and reinforcement.

There was notice for a meeting of property owners of East Point, Moore's Beach and Thompson's Beach to be held at Russ Sachleben's beach-front restaurant and boat livery at Thompson's Beach on June 9, 1963 at two o'clock P.M. It had to do with the township trying to pass an ordinance to abandon the three beaches. The township struggled financially with maintaining the roads for the beaches at that time.

There were interesting meeting minutes from a special meeting in 1969. It was a combination meeting with East Point and Thompson's Beach residents along with the local mayor and a representative from the Department of Navigation. The purpose was to discuss beach erosion and potential Federal aid in the matter. Mrs. Francis Robbins was there and spoke of their home being lost in the 1950 storm and the efforts that they had made prior to the storm to build up a bank to protect their place. There was discussion about the ditches that were dug by the Fish and Game Commission to drain the meadows. They asked the following questions. Will this form canals for both Thompson's Beach and East Point? Will it isolate both beaches? The residents were very concerned regarding these ditches.

There were some interesting notes in minutes from 1971 about when Captain Badger, owner of the speakeasy, cut off the water supply to James Buckley. It seems that Badger had been supplying water to Buckley's Boat Rental free of charge for three years from 1965 until he cut him off somewhere after 1968. There was discussion about how Jimmy Buckley would put in pipe and run water to his trailer and place of business.

The meeting minutes from the 1970's and 1980's reflected ongoing issues with pipe replacements and road maintenance, reconnection of street lights on Bay Avenue and issues with vandalism at beach properties.

By the late 1980's the membership fees had gone up to $50 per year for those still utilizing the water. Some houses had their own wells as time went on. Some of the resident names in the 1980's and 1990's were Corson, Cabaniss, Ferrell, Gatti, Mosier, Salloway, Sheer and St. Aubyn.

With the 1990's came some stringent regulations from the Department of Environmental Protection through Coastal Area Facility Review Act (CAFRA) which regulated coastal building requirements and waste water management. It presented some challenges for people wishing to build homes near the water.

From former beach resident, Mary Corson, I learned that the current keeper of the Association information is Paul Bijacsko, resident of East Point Beach. Per Paul, there are no longer monthly meetings like in the past. He still collects the dues for the year and the money is used to help neighbors if a pump or water line breaks. There is still that sense of community that has been a part of East Point for many decades.

BAD SANTA

There is an East Point Beach resident who sports a long white beard and is sometimes fondly referred to by the locals as Bad Santa or Pirate Paul. His given name is Paul Bijacsko. He started out at East Point about twenty-seven years ago with a trailer and a water-front location. Over a four-year period, he built a beautiful, clay-colored home that sits on pilings high above the ground with a beautiful view of the bay. As he recalled some of his favorite memories about the place that he calls home, he fondly shared the story that follows. Over time, Paul got to know a neighbor named Mike Penna. As they spent time together, he observed that Mike would always greet his sons by kissing them on the cheeks or forehead. Since Paul did not grow up in a family that was accustomed to such outward displays of affection, he was impressed by what he saw. Mike described it to him as the Italian way. Paul decided to start greeting his own son and daughter in this way. He found that the children liked it and it helped him to be more affectionate. He tells me that even though they are now grown up, he continues this loving display of affection with his children. It turns out that even bad Santa's can mend their ways.

This is a photograph of the home that was lovingly built by East
Point Beach resident, Paul Bijackso, over a four year period

EAST POINT FLAGPOLE STORY

Tom Wiechnik and Dick Secrest are the people responsible for the current flagpole that stands at the East Point Lighthouse. About fourteen years ago, the old flagpole, which had been erected thirty-five years earlier by two brothers from Leesburg, fell. The person responsible for the lighthouse at the time got an estimate to have it replaced for $5,000, so Tom and Dick offered to replace it themselves. They did it for a total cost of $250. They didn't charge for their services, as they wanted to give back to the community. They used a pipe their neighbor Dick Secrest already had and purchased additional piping from the junkyard. They assembled the pieces, painted the pole, and donated it to the lighthouse. Another former neighbor, Mr. Henderson, who lived along East Point Road, used his truck to help erect the flagpole, which former residents hope will stand for at least another couple of decades.

This photograph shows a side view of the East Point Lighthouse with a well-dressed man and young boy standing on a washed-out portion of the road circa 1960's. (Courtesy of Friends of the Lighthouse).

This is a view of the East Point Lighthouse taken on a boat excursion with our East Point neighbor, Captain Howard Langley, with passengers, Christina and Ed Longley, John Barone and Julie Rumbold. (Courtesy of Rumbold collection).

CAPTAIN HARRY BADGER'S PLACE

As local resident Sharon Johnson remembers, she used to go to Captain Badger's speakeasy at East Point as a child and had a lot of fun there. Sharon and her friends would sometimes ride their bicycles to Badger's, which she thought was just a restaurant where she could get ice cream as a reward for the long, hot ride. She would have to knock on the door, which was always locked, and Captain Badger would let them in. She didn't think anything of the security measure at the time. The captain would often be sitting in an easy chair with one of his hunting dogs on his lap. Sometimes Sharon would play a few games of pool with her friends, and she occasionally would go with her parents for a hamburger and fries. She recalls a unique stone fireplace there that Captain Badger built, which was decorated with an ornament of a sea captain that was bronze and had sort of a cut-out figure in the stone. She said it was really unusual. Sharon and I both recall a beautiful, big wooden ship on the mantle, and Sharon and her brother, Chick, remember the beautiful stone fireplaces Captain Badger, who made his living as a stonemason, built in the area. One of the last ones he did was in their neighbor's house, right down the street from the house where they grew up in Leesburg.

Chick says another local resident, Jimmy Camp, worked with the captain to build the fireplaces all around the area, including an awesome one in Libby's Last Stop. This was a popular bar along Route 47, just South of Millville, where the fireplace was very large and beautiful. My parents used to stop at Libby's on the way down to our cottage at Thompson's Beach. They would have a couple of beers, and my sister would play the jukebox and teach me how to dance.

TALES OF THE GRUFFS AND LEES, AS TOLD BY KAREN LEE

Karen Lee's mother-in-law, Carolyn Gruff, age ninety-nine and a half in 2016, spent a lot of springs and summers at East Point in her youth. Her father worked at Armstrong Glass in Millville and had a boat-rental place at East Point. They had a home there and also had a tent on the beach. Carolyn would still have to go up to Millville to high school until summer break, and her father would also commute to work in the city. Karen doesn't recall the name of the rental but suspects it was something uncomplicated, like "Gruff's Rentals."

Back in the 1940s, Carolyn would walk the beach from East Point to Thompson's Beach, because there was always something going on there. Typically, there was music to listen to and movies to see, and there were stores and souvenir shops. According to Karen, there was a movie theater at Thompson's Beach at the time. It was quite a beautiful and well-developed community at the time of World War II.

When Carolyn would walk as a teenager from one beach to the next, she would carry a bucket and fill it with blue claw crabs so plentiful she could just pluck them from the banks along the way. She would often meet a girlfriend whose last name was Butcher at Thompson's Beach. The girl was quite beautiful.

Carolyn met Karen's father-in-law, Charles ("Beanie") Lee, at Thompson's Beach. Apparently, Carolyn and her friend were at the part of the beach where the main road came in and met with the parking lot and bulkhead when a car came flying down the road and spinning in circles. Carolyn asked, "Who is that crazy man?"

Her friend replied, "Oh that's crazy Beanie Lee." Carolyn and Beanie ended up dating and eventually getting married; in fact, Charles proposed to Carolyn, and they were married the day before he was deployed in WWII. (Most able young men were in the service at that time.)

Captain Klein's Campground

People say beauty is in the eye of the beholder. Thankfully, we all have unique versions of what we perceive as beautiful; if that weren't the case, too many tourists would descend upon this "hidden paradise."

Nelson Klein has run Captain Klein's Campground at East Point since the mid-1980s. His parents bought the land in the 1950s and got a campground license in 1965. Interestingly enough, neither Nelson's father nor Nelson was a captain, but the nickname has stuck, since Nelson's grandfather ran Captain Klein's Rentals at Thompson's Beach. The family decided to carry on the name. Nelson owns a total of eighty acres of land, including ten acres across the East Point Road. A man named Mike DeFalco owned the land before the Kleins.

Nelson believes his campground is special because people look forward to coming there to relax and get away from it all (all the busyness of life and living). Originally, he says, transients used the campground, but it has become a place for more regulars or permanent campers now. A handful of campers used to come in; there were even tents at times, so the campers looked like nomads. There was a lot of sand there in the past to camp on.

Many former Thompson's Beach residents chose to come to Nelson's as they lost their cottages in storms. He says it seems like now the only way people leave is when they die—people really like this hidden paradise!

Another thing that has changed over the years is that there weren't any phragmitis weeds when the campground first opened. In fact, there weren't any phragmites in the area in the early 1960s, but when they arrived, they went crazy. As a kid, Nelson remembers his family going to the Catholic Church in Port Norris. He recalls seeing hundreds of muskrat houses on the sides of the road along the way. Now you can't spot them. They are still there, but you can't see them for all the weeds. Apparently, this weed is very invasive, with roots that are sometimes twenty feet long. Nelson says he heard someone brought phragmites from Europe to protect the banks of the Delaware River from erosion.

THE SHIPWRECK

According to Nelson, his father, Nelson Sr., worked at the Dorchester Shipyard as a sheet-metal-pattern drafter in the 1960s. At the time, two old wooden bunker boats had ended up at the shipyard after someone brought them down from the Hudson River in New York. Nelson isn't sure how or why they came to be there, but the shipyard owners decided to destroy them by sinking them on a reef or putting them on a bank somewhere. Nelson Sr. had an idea, and he asked for and ended up with one of the boats.

He decided to bring the boat to East Point in approximately 1967. His idea was to bring it down the creek and open it up as a luncheon-ette/sandwich store there on the river. Unfortunately, the tugboat that brought it down the river missed the tide, and the big wooden boat ran aground. That was where it stayed. The tugboat had to let it go and get out of there while it still could. The Klein family made several attempts to free the boat back when it still used to float. At times, Nelson and his dad attached one-inch cables to the boat, made a loop, and tried to walk it. They would also attach it to a "deadman," which was a piling submerged in the ground with another piling right behind it to make it stronger. They attached it to a big pulley on the front porch of a bungalow near the water, then tried to hand crank the winch to move the boat. Even with many attempts to free it, the large wooden boat stubbornly remained stranded on the beach.

Nelson recalls that when he was about ten years old, his dad got very sick with the Hong Kong flu. He remembers the water being across the road and a neighbor, Leon Riggins, coming down and telling his dad he had better get home and into bed to rest. Nelson offered to ride his bicycle down in order to crank the slack out of the cable that held the boat, but it had already run aground once again. That's where the boat has remained since, although at this point, there isn't much left of it.

Fortunately, for many years, the ship acted as a bulkhead to protect the beach and land from erosion. It also was and is a source of attraction to tourists, photographers, and artists. Its large wooden skeleton, anchored in the sand by the water's edge with beach grasses emerging from its bow is a thing of beauty. It's a reminder of times gone by when large boats were built by hand and entirely of wood. It is a clear demonstration of the power and destructiveness of nature. It is a spectacular sight when there are gorgeous sunsets, and streams of light illuminate its structure.

This depicts the sunken ship "The Fairmont" at Nelson Klein's campground as it appeared in the early 1970's. It was stranded on the beach in the late 1960's. (Courtesy of Nelson Klein).

East Point N.J., Ron Guida, Bay Ave, 25 Nov 2007

This beautiful home is located at East Point Beach. In 2007, it was owned by Ronald Guida. (Courtesy of Richard St. Aubyn).

Richard "Saint" St. Aubyn and His Son Rick St. Aubyn

● ● ●

Discovery at East Point Beach

In 1981, "Saint" and his wife, Rita, were just driving on Bay Avenue in East Point, New Jersey, when they saw bayfront property for sale. All that remained of the former home was a roof in the salt-hay meadow on the other side of the road. An unexpectedly powerful storm in 1980 had destroyed many homes at East Point and Thompson's Beach—the residents hadn't been prepared for it.

The St. Aubyns were struck by the beauty of the location, and eventually they decided to buy the then vacant lot. They didn't realize at the time the challenges they would face from the township and the Department of Environmental Protection (DEP). Initially, the township granted the St. Aubyns building permits, but then they rescinded them because the DEP challenged the type of septic system that was in place. Apparently, the regulations for waterfront septic systems had changed, and there were questions about whether the existing system was grandfathered, as was the case for the other homes that remained.

What followed was a six-year process of obtaining permission to build a home on their property at East Point Beach. The St. Aubyns filed a lawsuit with the township and the Department of Environmental Protection, trying to gain building and septic system permits. Once the DEP approved the existing septic system, the township finally granted them the permits in 1989. The lawsuit was then dropped. The St. Aubyns felt some hesitation to build after that because of all the trouble they had securing permits, but they eventually completed a small Cape Cod-style structure in

1996. Saint made his living as a contractor, so over time, he added to and improved upon the initial home. Today, there stands a beautiful structure with a cupola on top. There literally isn't a room without a view.

Rick says he likes this particular beach for its solitude and quiet—it isn't a crowed and noisy place like the ocean beaches in New Jersey. We all acknowledged that this sort of small bay community isn't for everyone, and Rick admits that when he first arrives, he is initially bored; after about thirty minutes, however, he is able to settle in and relax. He likes the varieties of nature at the beach; there are many types of seabirds and ducks, including cormorants. The bald eagles have returned as well. Apparently, they were absent for a time.

Full Moon over East Point Lighthouse, 24 Nov 2007, 6:30 AM

Here is a lovely view of the East Point Lighthouse taken from the St. Aubyn home on East Point Beach in 2007. (Courtesy of Richard St. Aubyn).

Horseshoe Crabs

● ● ●

I CANNOT WRITE A STORY about Thompson's Beach and East Point without including information about horseshoe crabs; they are an integral part of life at both places. In fact, they are a big part of the story at all the mid-Atlantic beaches. Horseshoe crabs are fascinating creatures. Although these creatures look like prehistoric crabs, and we *call* them crabs, they are not actually crabs. Interestingly, they are hard-shelled invertebrates more closely related to arachnids such as spiders and scorpions.

If you haven't seen a horseshoe crab, they are brown and have a hard outer shell, five pairs of legs, and gills for breathing. Their heads are rounded like a horseshoe (hence the name). They have nine sets of eyes, but only two are easy to spot in the front of their heads. They have long, pointy tails, called telsons, which they use for changing direction in the water and for flipping themselves upright if they get overturned in the waves. According to the National Wildlife Foundation, their appearance has changed little in three hundred million years. They predated the dinosaurs by two hundred million years! Scientists often call horseshoe crabs "living fossils," because fossils of their ancestors' date back close to four hundred fifty million years. They are daunting-looking creatures; however, they are harmless, unless you step on their tails in the sand.

Horseshoe crabs eat clams and worms in the water and are known for nesting in large groups on beaches in the mid-Atlantic states of New

Jersey, Delaware, and Maryland in the late spring and early summer. The females emit a type of pheromone to attract the males—it seems humans aren't the only ones who become attracted because of chemistry. Reportedly, most of the crabs' nesting activity takes place at night during high tides in the three days before and after a new moon or full moon. They are a vital part of the ecological system, as their eggs provide a major source of food for migratory birds. In fact, over half of the diet of many shorebirds consists of horseshoe-crab eggs.

In late May and throughout June, it is not uncommon to see pairs of horseshoe crabs attached to each other. The males, which are the smaller of the species by several inches, have special front claws to hook themselves to the back of the females. The females then lay their eggs in the sand at the water's edge, and the males fertilize the eggs. It is amazing to note that the female crabs lay eggs in clusters of four thousand eggs. They may spawn repeatedly and lay between twelve thousand and sixty thousand eggs at a time—and it's a good thing they do, because most horseshoe crabs will not even make it to the larval stage before being eaten. If an egg survives, the larval crab hatches between two to four weeks. The larvae look like miniature adults, minus the tail. As they grow, they shed their outer shells, which are rather soft when they are small, for larger, sturdier ones. It's interesting to note that horseshoe crabs do not reach full maturity or adulthood until they are ten years old. At that time, they start breeding. If they are fortunate, horseshoe crabs live to be about twenty years old.

Horseshoe crabs' blood is important to the biomedical industry, because it contains a substance that coagulates in the presence of toxins (poisons). Scientists use the blood, which is blue, to test the sterility of medical equipment and intravenous drugs. Live horseshoe crabs are also used to educate the public in aquariums and research labs. Unfortunately, the population of these sea creatures is rapidly declining for many reasons. Overdevelopment along the shoreline in the regions where they nest poses a threat to their mating habits, and horseshoe crabs have been used as bait to catch fish and eels in the past. To their detriment, it was discovered that they made good fertilizer as well. Their very survival depends on humans providing them with some protection and safe, unpopulated areas to reproduce.

SAVING MANY LIVES

As children, the Thompson's Beach and East Point Beach kids took it upon ourselves to save the horseshoe crabs, which we called "king crabs," one at a time. The summer children of Thompson's Beach would walk along the shore with our bare feet in the scorching sand and look for overturned crabs, which frantically moved their legs and claws in the air in futile attempts to right themselves, their gills moving rapidly to breathe. We would gingerly pick them up by their long, pointy tails and carry them to the water's edge; there, we would set them upright and watch them crawl rapidly back into the water to relative safety. If they remained overturned on the shoreline, they would become breakfast, lunch, or dinner for the seabirds. We did this all summer long, year after year, as we grew from small children to middle schoolers to high schoolers. We saved many lives in our early years.

If we had visiting friends from inland Pennsylvania, it was always fun to scare them by holding up a live king crab with the snapping claws and flapping gills facing them. We would have people screaming and running in no time.

The most horseshoe crabs were on the beach beginning in mid-May and continuing well into June. There were thousands of them. They would attach themselves to each other during mating season, and you would find them in pairs all along the beach. Then they would leave millions of tiny, greenish eggs buried in the sand near the water's edge. I remember the feel of them in my young fingers, and I recall the excitement of when the eggs would hatch, and we'd find tiny horseshoe crabs on the beach. Unfortunately, many perished in the waves.

Horseshoe Crabs during mating season at the edge of the water. In May and June there are thousands of horseshoe crabs on the beaches. (Courtesy of Rumbold Collection).

RETURNING THE FAVOR

Karen Lee participates in a program called Returning the Favor, which is all about "crab tipping." People volunteer to turn over horseshoe crabs that become stranded on their backs. This is a collaborative program in which the Wetlands Institute is a leading partner. In New Jersey, horseshoe crabs are protected by a moratorium, and Returning the Favor works closely with the New Jersey Division of Fish and Wildlife to save them. Karen went to a seminar and became certified as a leader in this movement, and she's required to report to the organization how many crabs are turned over and what each crab's sex is. In 2016, a lot of people volunteered in these tipping efforts. In fact, 78,041 horseshoe crabs along the Delaware Bay beaches were rescued in 2016. Karen obtained special permits to go to Thompson's Beach when it's closed between May 7 and June 7 each year, because red knots, an endangered shorebird, stop here to feed on horseshoe-crab eggs. If you scare the red knots, they won't eat. Karen's permits allow her to visit the beach between sunset and sunrise since the endangered birds are not feeding during this period, though she can go only at certain tides because the rough, unpaved road into Thompson's Beach floods.

Storm Stories

● ● ●

THE 1950 STORM SOME INSURANCE COMPANIES CLASSIFIED AS A TIDAL WAVE

THE DATE WAS NOVEMBER 25, 1950. In those days, there weren't the sophisticated weather-reporting methods that exist today. Nor was there a way to notify people quickly of impending disasters—cell phones and social media didn't exist—so there was no warning. According to Nelson Klein, who heard the stories from his parents, the tide never really went out that day. Instead, the tide came in on top of another tide, creating the perfect storm in the most horrible sense.

The storm came from the south. A spiraling pattern, it came with severe winds that some reported to be as fast as seventy-five miles per hour. Almost everyone had abandoned Thompson's Beach, because it was after the prime season; unfortunately, a few remained. Among them were Nelson's mother, Anna; his father, Nelson; his oldest sister, Mary Ann, who was about six months old at the time; and his grandfather, Adolfe.

Nelson's parents had an old dump truck at the beach, but they couldn't get out in time because of high waters over the road. As the storm intensified, Nelson's father realized they would need to move to higher ground to survive. Nelson Sr. moved with his wife and baby to the attic of their home. Eventually, the house started floating in the water, but it wouldn't move; something prevented it from floating away.

Apparently, it had become caught in the telephone wires. Nelson Sr. thought to take an old skillet to push the wires away from the upper part of the house. On the third hit, he managed to smack himself in the head with the frying pan and cut his head open, but he also managed to free the house from the tangle of wires. Their house floated a reported half to three-quarters of a mile to the outskirts of Heislerville, finally landing near a pond that no longer exists and a road that leads to East Point.

Since the 1930s, Adolfe Klein had owned a thriving general store called Captain Klein's Boat Rentals at Thompson's Beach. Nelson's grandfather didn't want to abandon the store, so he stayed there, hoping to wait out the storm. Until that time, there was a pier, and Adolfe had fishing boats for rent. He used to sell hand-dipped ice cream, grilled burgers, groceries, and bait for the plentiful fishermen. There was a penny arcade with pinball machines. On Friday nights, the locals would meet up there to socialize, play banjos and guitars, and dance to music. In fact, according to Nelson, there were about seven boat rentals at Thompson's Beach at the time. The captain stayed with his store on that November day and lost his life when the roof collapsed.

Nelson Klein Sr. told people the water was halfway up the telephone poles at Thompson's Beach that early Saturday morning. He wanted to leave, but his father told him he would never get out. The water was too deep to leave.

Nelson remembers one other human fatality, plus the death of a pig, from the storm. He says the woman who died was Mrs. Lee, but he doesn't recall her first name. The stories he heard were that she managed to hand either her children or her grandchildren off the porch to a rescuer. Reportedly, she was a large woman and couldn't get around too well, so she perished in the storm, along with her pet pig.

Coincidentally, Nelson's parents had taken a long walk on the beach on November 24, 1950, and counted all the houses. That day they'd counted 107 homes. Two days later, only seven houses remained.

Some of the destruction from the 1950 storm can be seen in these pictures from Thompson's Beach. (Courtesy of Nelson Klein).

A Blowout Tide

Drew Tomlin, who lives in the local town of Leesburg, says the 1950 storm had what was called a "blowout tide." Apparently, there had been a strong northwesterly wind blowing for about three days before the devastating storm occurred, so the high tide came up only to where low tide would be normally. Suddenly, the wind direction shifted, and a strong easterly wind pushed a wall of water ahead of it. Some people reported it as a tidal wave.

Explorer Scouts at East Point Lighthouse during the 1950 Storm

Per local resident, Bob Frantz, a group of Boy Scouts, called the Explorer Scouts, asked the state, which owned the East Point lighthouse at the time, for permission to camp there for the weekend. They got approval, if they agreed to do some service work while they were there. They consented to some painting and set out with their scout leader, who drove them there but did not stay, for a fun weekend at the lighthouse. Little did they know that a huge storm was coming. As the night went on, one of the scouts had a battery-operated radio, and they could hear high winds. Bob didn't sleep much that night. He watched the flag pole outside the lighthouse and used it to gauge how high the tide was rising. The water came all the way up to the first floor of the lighthouse but did not come inside the door. Nonetheless, the boys said they could hear water pouring into the basement. It continued to climb the cellar steps until it reached the fourth step from the top. It was a frightening time for a bunch of young boys. They were essentially stranded at the lighthouse. There was also a group of very worried parents in the surrounding villages as the magnitude of the storm was revealed.

In the morning, they were surprised to see at least five houses from Thompson's Beach floating by like boats on the bay in front of the lighthouse. They could see flowers on kitchen tables as the houses sailed by. Some of them, being young boys, took to shooting out the windows of the floating targets with their BB guns. Houses were floating everywhere; they also ended up on East Point Road and in the salt-hay meadows that surrounded the beach communities. Bob said they were concerned for a while that some of them would smash into the lighthouse. Some floated as far as three miles from Thompson's Beach to the village of Delmont. Bob was also concerned that the large boat stored in the barn out back would crash into their save haven.

This is a group of Explorer Scouts at the East Point Lighthouse. Some of these boys may have been the ones who were camping there when the November storm of 1950 struck. (Courtesy of Drew Tomlin).

New Home for a Home

Many of the houses that floated from their foundations found new resting places along Glade and East Point Roads in Heislerville, where they remain today. In fact, Kit and Lou Peterson, told me that Kit's parents' Thompson's Beach cottage ended up a car length off East Point Road, facing the road as if it was supposed to be there and with an outhouse conveniently placed beside it.

Loss of Life

Thirteen people lost their lives in the storm of 1950. It was particularly devastating to Thompson's Beach and another bay community nearby at Moore's Beach where one family alone lost four young children in the frigid November waters.

Hurricane Doria

The date was August 28, 1971. I was a teenager at the time, and what I remember is this: It was strangely quiet in the early evening. There were no cricket sounds. The seagulls seemed to have disappeared. No sandpipers danced along the shoreline. Nature wasn't making a sound. It was as though the creatures had a sixth sense. They knew something dangerous was lurking in the not-too-distant future, and the stillness was eerie. I remember standing out on our pier over the water. There wasn't any breeze blowing; in fact, the air was perfectly still. Prior to this, I had never experienced that particular kind of silence, but I knew something was amiss. There had been warnings of a storm—I recall someone from town coming later to warn the residents that they should leave.

My family was staying at our beach house that summer, as was our custom. Mom always had everything packed up the day we got out of school, and we would leave Parkside, Pennsylvania, for Thompson's Beach, where we would stay until Labor Day.

My dad would come for the weekends and for vacation, and we were all there that day with our dog, Whiskers. After some discussion, we decided to divide up and go stay with a few different friends in Heislerville.

At some point, a few hours later, it seemed as though the storm had passed. My parents and another neighbor, Larry Pinto, decided to return to the beach. Apparently, as we would find out later, it was just the eye of the storm. Mom, Larry, and Whiskers left shortly after Dad and ended up trapped on Delaware Avenue (the gravel road that led into the beach). They had made it about halfway to our cottage when the dog started to whimper and climbed up into the ledge by the car's rear windshield.

As Mom told it the next day, the water suddenly seemed to flow across the road from both the bay and the canal that ran behind the houses. She recalled seeing a refrigerator floating in the water in front of the car. Mom and Larry knew they couldn't drive any farther. The water started to enter the car, and they needed to get to a safe place. Mom was terrified, because she didn't know how to swim. She was very lucky that Larry was a large man who was actually a Philadelphia Mummer; he held on to her and led her to the closest house through waist-high water. For those who are not from the Philadelphia area, the Mummers New Year's Day Parade is believed to be the oldest, continuous folk parade in the United States. Local clubs design and create elaborate costumes and compete in different categories including comics, fancy, string band, and brigades.

The home's door was locked, and Larry had to break it in. Mom held on to an outside light while he did this, and apparently, she got a shock when he turned on the switch. They were not in the house long before the waves began crashing against the front windows. When the windows started to break, they climbed the stairs to the second story. That's where they stayed until they were rescued.

In the meantime, Dad had made it back to our cottage. Apparently, he needed to use the restroom and was in a hurry to get back to the house. He parked the car on the gravel driveway next to the cottage; went to the bathroom; and then sat on the couch, where he fell asleep. He missed most of the storm and was awakened by people banging on the door to take him out by boat. I guess I should mention at this point that he had been drinking prior to heading back to the cottage. Dad had no idea that Mom and Larry had made it as far as the beach, or that they had to be rescued as well. We lost two cars in that storm, but our dog survived.

I had left the beach to stay with a friend who lived in Heislerville. We decided to take a ride back down Thompson Beach Road to see what was happening, and what we saw was quite frightening. We parked the car along the blacktop road and got out. We could see waves breaking over the telephone lines at the entrance to the beach, and there was a lot of wind. We could see water spouts spinning along the flooded road from the ferocity of the storm. Other locals had gathered in the same area to witness the horrific storm. We heard that people needed to be rescued, but we had no idea at the time that those people were my parents and Larry. The emergency response personnel told us to leave.

When we headed for the beach the next day, we saw carnage. Large portions of the gravel road were completely gone. Parts of houses were washed away. Furniture and appliances sat in the middle of what had been the road. I remember being shocked by all the wreckage.

Our Buick Electra remained where it had stopped on the road. It was filled with mud and debris. Our second car, a Ford Galaxy, was turned on its side next to our cottage, which still stood because it sat up high on pilings.

THE KRUPAS DURING HURRICANE DORIA

As Ed Krupa tells it, he and his family were all at Tommy's cottage as Hurricane Doria approached. He remembered hearing that a bad storm was predicted and was coming up the bay. Since most of the residents at the beach were used to waiting out storms, they planned to stay and eventually went to bed for the night. They were awakened by the sound of howling winds and splashing waters. The tide was extremely high. They knew that it would be prudent to leave the beach. They tried to drive their vehicles out but were stranded in high water and unable to proceed very far from the house. They decided to walk out. The Krupas' youngest children were twins named Trisha and Eddie. They were just small children at the time. Ed and Tommy each carried a twin on their shoulders as they all struggled together through the swirling water that completely covered the gravel lane. They made it to the blacktop road that led into Thompson's Beach. Everyone in Ed and Tommy's family made it to safety, but they lost two cars and a truck in the deep waters.

TOMMY WIECHNIK'S MEMORIES OF THE 1980 STORM

Tommy had been drinking, and he was sound asleep when a neighbor, Les Myers, banged on his door. Tommy's dog, Anchor, started barking, which helped to wake him up. Les was yelling, "Leave the damn beach, Tommy." When Tommy looked out his door, he saw everything was flooded. One of his nephews who was staying at the beach house told him the waves were over the road, and they needed to get out fast. Some of the neighbors' cars were swamped, but a couple of people did manage to get out. Ed Krupa and Tommy both recalled that family members were carrying young children on their shoulders and tried to put them in a car. They got as far as opening the car door before a huge wave filled the vehicle. The only way out at that point was to walk, so that's what they did.

There were a few bad storms before that, according to Tommy, but the 1980 storm was the worst one he remembered. Sometime before that summer, his house had been by the beach, but he had moved it across the street and a little farther from the bay. Apparently, one of his neighbors, Bert Lipstick, wouldn't agree to move her house. She didn't want to lose her view of the bay—Tom laughed about this, because he had an excellent view, even across the road. Unfortunately, during the 1980 storm, waves blew Bert's house down. He recalled that the waves hit it "just like a mud ball," while the wave surge just missed his house.

THE 2012 STORM

It was a quiet, peaceful night when the St. Aubyn family went to sleep, but that would change unexpectedly during the night. Per Saint and Rita

St. Aubyn's son Rick, the storm that occurred on December 22, 2012, was worse for his parents' home on Bay Avenue in East Point than Hurricane Sandy had been just months earlier. At three o'clock that morning, Rick's mom called him at his home in Malaga, New Jersey, from East Point. She told him she was standing on the deck in front of their beach home. Both the house and deck stand about ten feet from the ground. She said it felt like she was standing on a speedboat. The wind was fierce, and the waves had crashed over the front bulkhead.

The road was completely covered with rushing water. Waves crashed over the St. Aubyns' car, which they'd parked behind the house near what used to be the road. The bay water was flowing into the marsh on the other side of Bay Avenue, and there was nothing Rick could do to save his parents. He was afraid for them, because it was a bad storm. They were completely trapped with no way out. No rescue workers would have risked their lives trying to get to them through high winds and flooded roads buried beneath quickly moving streams of water.

Fortunately for Saint and his wife, their house survived the ferocity of this unexpected storm, though their two vehicles did not fare as well. One car, which was only two years old at the time, sank down into the ground. They got it out, started it and managed to get it to their homestead in Malaga, but that evening, the horn started blowing all by itself and wouldn't stop until the battery finally died. The electronics in the floor had gotten wet and were beyond salvaging. The St. Aubyns also had a truck that was totaled by the flood. In fact, everything outside their beach home was lost: Their propane tank floated over to the meadow off East Point Road. All their beautiful sea glass, which they displayed in a container outside their home, floated away. Their heavy metal boat and motor floated to the road over by Captain Klein's Campground, where it still remains.

Saint's grandsons, Stevie and Mike, drove down as far as they could in the early morning hours and said that water was everywhere. According to Saint, the beach lost more than a foot of dirt and gravel in that sudden and furious storm. After this harrowing event, Saint and his wife always left the beach if there were serious storm predictions. As he says, things can get bad within a half hour with the right combination of wind, tide, and moon.

This cottage once sat at the very end of Thompson's Beach toward Moore's Beach. It looks as if it was about to crumble into the water when this was taken. (Courtesy of Ed Krupa).

This photograph was taken from the St. Aubyn home at East Point when the tide was high and the wind was strong one morning in 2007. (Courtesy of Richard St. Aubyn).

East Point was struck hard by two storms in 2012. The one that occurred in October and was the cause of this destruction was Hurricane Sandy. An un-named storm also happened in December of that year and caused significant damage. (Courtesy of Richard St. Aubyn).

Fast-Forward

• • •

NOTHING REMAINS OF THOMPSON'S BEACH these days, save for a paved blacktop road that passes through flooded salt-hay meadows with eerie, dead trees; a couple of osprey nests; a raised wooden platform for bird-watchers with an inlet behind it; and a barricade blocking a rocky, unpaved road that leads to sand and water. A beautiful stone fireplace still stands near the beach and a section of bulkhead remains. It is a great place to take a long walk at low tide, witness the nothingness of the present, and imagine what it must have been like when there was a thriving community that once boasted more than one hundred homes. Thompson's Beach is now one of Maurice River Township's lost villages.

East Point Beach has survived, however. It is the home of the historic East Point Lighthouse, the second-oldest lighthouse in New Jersey. Friends of the Lighthouse have made gallant efforts to restore East Point Lighthouse to its original beauty and to protect it from significant encroaching erosion. The Maurice River Township Heritage Society is also working to preserve the significant history of the area. If you haven't visited this lovely rural spot, plan a trip. It's worth the effort to experience the beauty and solitude of this bayside community.

There are frequent bald eagle sightings at East Point Beach. This one seems to be posing for the picture by a neighbor's home on the water. (Courtesy of John Barone).

This is a view of East Point Lighthouse from East Point Beach. This spectacular landmark is a beautiful sight to behold. (Courtesy of Christina Longley).

Here the sea gulls are seen feasting on horseshoe crab eggs near the sunken ship. This is a typical scene in early summer. (Courtesy of Julie Rumbold).

In this photograph, Christina Longley is relaxing by the water and watching her husband, Ed, catch fish in a net. (Courtesy of Rumbold collection).

Author's nephew Ronald Flynn is standing at the entrance to the long, rocky road leading to Thompson's Beach. (Courtesy of J. Rumbold).

ABOUT THE AUTHOR

• • •

As a child, Julie Ann Rumbold spent every summer at Thompson's Beach in Maurice River Township, New Jersey. She cherishes those memories, but due to both environmental and political factors, the beach no longer exists. She lovingly preserves her past and the local lore of that special spot with *High Tide, Full Moon, and Fading Memories.*

In 2016, Rumbold retired from her long career as a registered nurse and health care recruiter. She is married to John Barone and has adult children, Adam Valenzano and Ryan McClellan and stepchildren, Kristen and Kimberly Barone.